TOOLS FOR CAREGIVERS

- **F&P LEVEL:** C
- **WORD COUNT:** 37

- **CURRICULUM CONNECTIONS:** nature, seeds, flowers

Skills to Teach

- **HIGH-FREQUENCY WORDS:** a, are, big, I, in, is, it, see, the, them, this, we, will
- **CONTENT WORDS:** bud, grow(s), middle, opens, petals, plant, seed(s), stem, sunflower, water, yellow
- **PUNCTUATION:** exclamation points, periods
- **WORD STUDY:** compound word (*sunflower*); long /e/, spelled ee (*see, seed*); long /o/, spelled ow (*grows, yellow*)
- **TEXT TYPE:** information report

Before Reading Activities

- Read the title and give a simple statement of the main idea.
- Have students "walk" through the book and talk about what they see in the pictures.
- Introduce new vocabulary by having students predict the first letter and locate the word in the text.
- Discuss any unfamiliar concepts that are in the text.

After Reading Activities

Explain to readers that "sunflower" is a compound word. This means its name is made up of two different words: "sun" and "flower." Ask readers how they think sunflowers got their name. What do sunflowers look like? Then ask readers if they can name any other flowers or plants that are compound words. Write their answers on the board.

Tadpole Books are published by Jump!, 5357 Penn Avenue South, Minneapolis, MN 55419, www.jumplibrary.com

Copyright ©2023 Jump. International copyright reserved in all countries. No part of this book may be reproduced in any form without written permission from the publisher.

Editor: Jenna Gleisner **Designer:** Molly Ballanger

Photo Credits: Olaf Simon/Shutterstock, cover; Ian 2010/Shutterstock, 1; Shutterstock, 2mr, 3; vladdon/Shutterstock, 2ml, 4; PavelRodimov/iStock, 2br, 5; Spooxy/Shutterstock, 2bl, 6–7; thala bhula/Shutterstock, 2tl, 8–9; Teri Virbickis/Shutterstock, 10–11; Sergio33/Shutterstock, 2tr, 12–13; saroch/Shutterstock, 14–15; nelya43/Shutterstock, 16.

Library of Congress Cataloging-in-Publication Data
Names: Sterling, Charlie W., author.
Title: Sunflower / by Charlie W. Sterling.
Description: Minneapolis, MN: Jump!, Inc., (2023) |
Series: See a plant grow! | Includes index. | Audience: Ages 3–6
Identifiers: LCCN 2021047401 (print) | LCCN 2021047402 (ebook)
ISBN 9781636907055 (hardcover)
ISBN 9781636907062 (paperback)
ISBN 9781636907079 (ebook)
Subjects: LCSH: Sunflowers—Life cycles—Juvenile literature.
Classification: LCC SB413.S88 S74 2023 (print) | LCC SB413.S88 (ebook) | DDC 583/.983—dc23
LC record available at https://lccn.loc.gov/2021047401
LC ebook record available at https://lccn.loc.gov/2021047402

SEE A PLANT GROW!

SUNFLOWER

by Charlie W. Sterling

TABLE OF CONTENTS

Words to Know 2

Sunflower 3

Let's Review! 16

Index 16

WORDS TO KNOW

bud

petals

plant

seed

stem

water

SUNFLOWER

seed

This is a
sunflower seed.

I plant it.

I water it.

stem

A stem grows!

It grows big.

bud

I see a bud.

It opens.

petal ·····▶

The petals are yellow.

seed

Seeds grow in the middle.

14

We will plant them!

LET'S REVIEW!

Sunflowers start as seeds. They grow seeds, too. Where do a sunflower's seeds grow?

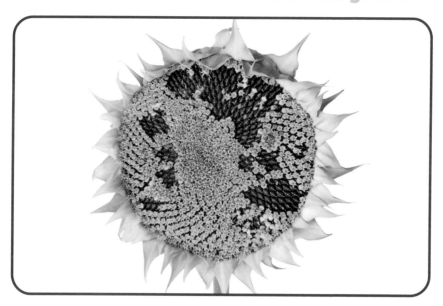

INDEX

bud 9

petals 13

plant 4, 15

seed 3, 14

stem 7

water 5